Printed in the United States of America

Dedication

To God who gets the honor and glory, without you this definitely wouldn't have been possible . To my husband who supported me following my dreams. To my children,family and friends, thank you. This book of poems was born from the day to day life situations that impact faith. While I know that without faith it is impossible to please God, there are many days where faith needs to be renewed . Life is not easy, take comfort in knowing your journey is your own but you are not alone.

Faith is our armory
Hope is our battle plan
Love is our weapon
Compassion is our Arsenal
Humility is our defense

Faith

Faith is suppose to be all things unseen
But what if that's not true
I bet you are wondering what I mean
I have faith that is a mile wide

I have seen things, miracles working in my life
Shaping and forming like a beautiful painting
When I look faith shows me what I thought I
would never see

When I listen I hear things I thought would
never come to be
When I feel I have a peace underneath it all
I have assurance and knowledge of one who
conquers all

Take My Hand

Take my hand,
Hold it tight and stay with me
Never look down or backwards, there's nothing
there to see
Wipe those tears, from your eyes
I am there with you
Seeing what you don't see and how you will
make it through
Cease those words of condemnation and of self
doubt
Speak of your mighty future and how you make
it out

Believe and walk in faith and trust the Lord
For he is always faithful and sticks to his word
For he said he loves you and you will always be
A child who's father is a king

God's promises

Although I'm not where I want to be
spiritually
I know there are others taking their own
journey with me
Walking with God learning his word
Finding the path that God has designed

I fall sometimes in the temptation of sin
It's hard to resist I try not to give in
Because I can glimpse what he sees in me
When the clouds briefly clear
I see the talents and beauty he has designed
in me

I want it to shine
I want it to shout
I want it to grow
I want to bring it out
I want the whole wide world to know
It's because of his goodness
Whom all of my blessings flow

You can have him as well there's enough to
go around
He loves you too, just like me
He's placed in you unique talents and beauty
It's yours alone not made for me
It's designed for you, it's yours to see

Take 1% of how much God believes in you
It's enough to make sure that what you aspire
to comes true
Take 1% of God's faith in you
You'd conquer the world there's nothing you
couldn't do
Take 1% of God's love for you
You'd weep with joy feeling love so consuming
Take 1% of God's forgiveness for you
You'd make peace with everyone who has
ever hurt you

I took 1% faith and it was enough for me to
see
That God is God
His word is truth
His promises will all come to be
So I know if I fall God will pick me up
That he is enough to fill my cup
If I slow down , he will keep pace
That he will be at the finish line when I am
done with this race

Hope

Hope is lost
It got caught up and tied down by sorrow,
regret and pain
The new rules of the future make hope not
want to appear again

Where the news, violence, senseless acts and
hate bombards us everyday
It's hard to find hope wanting to mix in with
the fray
It could appear if we let it but that would
mean that we would have to let it in

It would have to reside in us for hope to truly
begin
To be birthed into our nations, our society and
in our homes
Hope doesn't want to live in a residence where
it's all alone

So build it and plant it and allow it to grow
Give it rich soil and fertilizer just to let it
know
That you're here with hope for the long haul
That you will resist the temptation of defeat
when it calls

Hope lets you see a better tomorrow
Even though the vision could be murky and foggy
It's still a direction for you to take
To start to leave your current circumstances in
your wake

If it's not hope for you, I could use some more
you see
We all could use more hope in our society
The benefits of hope outweigh its harm
If you have no hope you can't believe in anyone

If there is hope the world has more potential
More possibilities, outcomes and solutions to tap
into
It gives you a river to pull from
A place to rest and part of the spiritual
nourishment that you need
Hope can be a pretty powerful core rock in deed

Don't take me at my word and try it on so that
you can see
Hope is powerful and gives you a reason to
believe
I hope you heard me and will answer my call
To allow hope back in, which will benefit us all

Faith

I'm conflicted in my faith
I feel like I hide my faith away
When I do, it makes me want to cry
Crying because hiding allows my faith to die

Faith in truth means I have to walk in my faith
Never ever hiding or putting my faith away
Walking boldly believing in his word

Falling on my knees, so I can hear
The sweetest voice who draws me near
He tells me without faith it's impossible to be
All the things that he sees in me

For I can't please God by hoping for the best
For only with faith can my soul find rest
Faith that he sent his son for me
Helping to erase my iniquities
Faith that he wants to be
In a one on one love relationship with me

Faith that he'll guide me if I lay my concerns
down in prayer
Faith that he'll pick them up and lead me from
there
Faith that my tears are not in vain
Because his grace and mercy will forever reign

Faith that he is constant and never changing
Always forgiving and never blaming
While that doesn't mean there are not
consequences to my acts
He picks me up and says welcome back

From that place I didn't want to be
I cried out Lord don't depart from me
I am nothing but sin without you there
Wearing a buyer beware sign, cause only death
lives here
Without you residing in my soul, my soul would
only have one place to go

I want you Lord but clearly you wanted me first
You showed me before I was born what you
thought I was worth
You said you didn't want me to perish or be
apart from you
So you sent your son with a life changing task
to do

Thank you Lord for the gift of faith
For with this faith I'm surrounded by you
Living, breathing and residing in me
Catching my spirit in death because I chose to
believe
That you are the truth, the light, the life for all
those who believe

God's plan

My story is not over, matter fact its just
beginning
This is a new chapter and the last chapter is
finally ending

You would have thought I was in a drama, a
mystery, maybe a horror show
It was hard to see it is a story about resilience
and hope

All I know is that I'm entering the chapter
where blessings flow
Where I still will have trials and tribulations
but I know who holds me close

Where I still may have heartache and pain,
today is different, circumstances have changed

What has changed is what I let inside of me,
who I surround myself with and who I choose
to be
I choose to be a survivor, a woman of truth and
a loving mother

But beyond these things I use faith as my cover
It's surrounds me, it's in me, it carries me
It keeps me focused on those things I can't see
Like God's amazing love for me

I know he loves me because I wouldn't be where
I am today
I would not have found this path, he wouldn't
have let me know that I had gone astray
He showed me a different path, he says it is
yours to take
So I took the first step and he still hasn't left
yet

So while my world is different and I have much
clarity
I know there are still trials and tribulations
waiting in the world for me
But there's also joy and fulfillment and God's
plan for me
And having his plan tells me I can be what he
wants me to be

Hope and Resiliency

Side by side they stand together
Inseparable through disappointment and pain
Leaning on one another time and time again
Resiliency saying defeat won't win
It wants you to stay down there
It wants you to pretend
That there is no other place you can go
There are no other solution, defeat is all you'll know

Hope saying I really do believe
If we hang together, all things we can achieve
I won't give up on you, if you don't give up on me
I see a vision of the future and I know if you'll stand
with me

That our future will come to pass, that our present will
no longer be
Pick me up whenever I stumble and fall
Give me assurance to remember that there is no failure
at all
Only refinements until it comes to pass
Each lesson learned gives new information to grasp

Resiliency needing a seed to begin
A seed of hope that lets a new future in
No matter the circumstance or what's in front of you
Carry these two things with faith and all things are
possible

Believe In Your <u>Purpose</u>

It was God's gift to me
It was my purpose, my destiny
He gave it to me on my birthday you see
It was there the day I came in this world, the day
I came to be

He told me it is yours to give
It's inside you it's the place that I live
Where your heart, spirit and faith coincide
It's in that place I reside

When you opened up and you let me in
You gave a way for your talents to begin
To show up when you are walking your path
When you build your relationship with God you'll
be shown all you have

Not just all you have but all he has to give
All the blessing and lessons when you walk with
him
It's amazing that it was there all this time
That it was waiting for me to recognize what was
mine

So believe, believe and believe some more
You'll be amazed at what knocks at your door
Destiny, purpose, impact and a relationship that
will last test of time
It's yours take it , don't leave it behind

Be a leader in me

My vision for the world is that they find me
That we are reconciled for all eternity
That their sins are forgiven if they trust in me
That my promises will all come to be

For Satan didn't believe in that vision, so
He tempted man to create a division
Showed them knowledge that didn't come with wisdom
So that man could die without reconciliation

But there is only one leader and I'm in control
All your trials and tribulations and your heart I know
Each and everyday I watch your trust in me grow
Each and everyday new wisdom unfolds

I've given you a gift of mercy and grace
I ask that you trust in me and keep the faith
For out of faith births goodness and knowledge of me
With growing knowledge self control you can achieve
Self control helps you conquer the desires of man
Helps you persevere,endure and to continue to stand

For then you are standing in my word and my grace
You are standing in the promises I have made to the
human race
Within those promises you have built a heart to serve
For you a leader now cause you know your worth

For I sent a precious gift so that you could return to me
I want you to share the good news with those that don't
believe
For your mission is to help others return to me
Let them know the promises made to all who believe

Sharing how my mercy and grace has allowed you to stand
Sharing how I've always had a special love for man
For you were created in my image and my image alone
I breathed in you spiritual life before you were born

I wanted you to recognize who dwells in thee
That I'm the truth, the light, the father to all those who
believe
You are wonderfully and fearfully made
You were given gifts, talents and purpose to share with the
human race

For in your serving and giving you are a leader in me
I will always provide every tool you ever need
Know that I will give you the words, the abilities and my
message to share
Know that your tears don't fall on deaf ears cause I'm
always there

Know that you can stand with your head held up high
Because you are bathed in forgiveness with no
condemnation in my eyes
So go forward with purpose , destiny and grace
So go forward sharing the good news about the author of
your faith

I will hold you and comfort you and always be there
All you need to do is lay your burdens down in prayer
Then hold fast because I will always take it from there

Your Center

"My grace is sufficient for you, for my power is made perfect in weakness. Therefore I will boast all the more gladly about my weaknesses, so that Christs power may rest on me. That is why, for Christ's sake, I delight in weaknesses, in insults, in hardships,in persecutions, in difficulties. For when I am weak, then I am strong.

Your center is your weakness, that's where your strength lies
It's when you let go and cry out to our God that your strength arises
For in your darkness and deepest despair, call out to God and he is there
You are not alone, never, for he cares for you and loves you so
For you may not hear or see him but he always holds you close

For the winds may blow and sway you
Making you feel like you are unsteady
But in the moments you are moving, to where God is getting you ready

For your life mate is your anchor, whom God led you to
For he is preparing you both for glory and the work he has for you
So lay down in your weakness, your situation and your circumstance
Because when you lay down, you are resting in his mighty hands

No need to wonder if you are lost and where do you go from here
No need to hold it together, because God knows what you fear
Please rest with peace and give God your burdens
Give him the confusion, the despair and all those things that are hurting

Then take a deep breath of relief and inhale in God's truth
That no person nor weapon, will take away what he is preparing for you
Because it is preparation, it's enhancement, not defeat
For soon you will turn a corner, to find the generational curses laying at your feet

Musing of the Soul

I'm writing because I feel the need to write
I don't know what to write but I sit here with a
feeling that needs to be born
Birth is interesting process because its creation
Creation of an idea or concept that is now
realized
A thought that leads to reality
Sometimes birth takes the form of a creature or
being
Sometimes birth is an idea for a new innovation
Sometimes birth is the discovery of ones self
To be born again over and over is a good thing
It means you're not stuck in how you are living
You can be born again over and over again
Just pick up the stick marked forgiven
Don't take it for granted and keeping straying
away
Because one day being reborn wont be an option
Work on being born because then there is change
and acknowledgment that birth is the only way
To start fresh and new when you stray away
Pray pray pray

Lord thank you

Lord thank for you loving me
Thank you so much for your grace and mercy
For I believe In You lord more and more each and
everyday
Thank you for never leaving me and helping grow my
faith
You are awesome, amazing, beautiful in your love for
me
You continue to reward my walking in faith and
obedience
In this moment I shout hallelujah, praise God, bless his
holy name
I can't get over your love for me and my fellow man
I sit here in awe and at peace believing you cover me
I sit here in awe the gifts and purpose you have for me
You shine upon my life this very day
Lighting my path and slowly showing me your Godly
way
I thank you, I thank you for never giving up on me
Showing me my path through the things I can achieve
Cause of you all things are possible in my life
Cause of you I finally take back what's mine
It was a gift from you so long ago
One I recognize today as my very own
Thank you God, I praise your holy name
In Jesus name I give thanks today

Growing up amongst the weeds

Sometimes it's hard sharing space with weeds
They clog my space absorbing nutrients I need
Growing faster and bigger everyday single day
They look like they are prospering having little hope or
faith

But the Gardener sees and knows what is really
growing
Come harvest time, the weeds are left there burning
No matter how big they are, ashes is what their turning
So I need to stay in my place of prayer and enduring

The weeds get the same sunshine to help them grow
The weed share the same soil so they should know
But they don't because they eat a different food
Not knowledge and truth but lies is what they chew

Sometimes it's ignorance, or doubt they hold on to
If I don't hold on to truth and light I just might believe
That I'll be choked and suffocated, swallowed up by the
weeds
The master gardener gives me grace and mercy
It's the same opportunity the weeds get to have
The only difference is I chose to grab it

Weeds are still beautiful if you take a different view
The view of the master gardener who can wash them
anew
It's not too late, it's not over because they still have
time
Time to change before the harvest or be left behind

It's not my place to judge but only to pray
Pray a prayer of thanksgiving for his mercy and
grace
Pray for the others, who could be saved just like me
If the shed their doubts, plant a seed of faith and just
believe

For God gave us a seed that can grow and be
multiplied
With the nutrients from the Holy Spirit that will help
faith thrive
Growing up amongst the weeds is not a bad thing
It only amplifies the joy that Gods presence brings

The Master Gardener has a request, that we tend the
weeds
He wants us to change lives, helping weeds to become
seeds
For seeds multiply and can bear fruit
Spreading his message of forgiveness, light, knowledge
and truth

So know, you are planted where he wants you to be
For the only to do his work is to be next to the weeds

Step into the fire

Step into the fire and feel the flames
It burns away your grime and sinning ways
It exposes what's buried underneath
The hurt, rejection, pain and defeat

It engulfs those things that don't come from me
Leaving you open and exposed to new ways of being
In those new ways, new life can be born
New purpose, new learnings with meaning can be
formed

No need to cry , feel lost or mourn
For in the fire you can cast your sins
Knowing that they can judged to die, never to rise
again

Then I'll give to you a fire that will dwell in thee
Helping you to gain new knowledge and wisdom of me
Helping you to call out and cast all your cares on me
Knowing that I hear you and I will never leave

For my fire is a good thing and my burden light
It can burn away hurt and rejection in your life
For I want to always be there and dwell in thee
I've wanted you since the beginning of time to be with
me

For with this fire , it gives you the power to be
Victorious, walking in dominion, not believing defeat
Cause victory is ours, this battle has already been
won
It was finished that day by my begotten son

However you are still on the battle field
There is more work to be done
There are more lives to be saved that don't know me
There are people that don't know I AM everything
they need

So step into the fire and stay in the fire, praying day
and night and
I will continue to pour into you my flame of life

It's not easy, I know it's not easy but I know one
thing for sure
The fire will give your spirit the food it needs to
endure
Not just endure but mature to a whole new level
Giving you faith and confidence to thwart the devil

He wants you to believe that your pain, hurt,
disappointments are the way you'll end
That you'll stay in darkness shying away because of
your sins

But in the flame comes forgiveness and the burning
light
That lets you shine and the world know your a child
of mine
So shine in the flames, shout hallelujah and let the
devil see
That those that step in the fire are now home with
me

All Praise

So today we celebrate and remember what God
had done
Sending us the ultimate sacrifice, his only
begotten son
Rejoice, rejoice and remember that this is good
news
Remember Jesus's suffering and all that he
went through
Because when he died on the cross he was
thinking of you
Yes you and me and all of humanity
He died and rose so that we might live again
So give thanks and praise to the one who loves
us so
So give thanks and praise to the one who holds
us close
So give thanks and praise for his love and
grace
So give thanks and praise because our
redeemer lives today
For this isn't history it's our present where
God is alive
Look around the room because he lives in you
and I
So all praise to our redeemer, our God for
sending his son
For going to prepare a place for us so that we
can be as one

My Disease

Today is a beautiful day but the clouds are
rolling in
I'm supposed to get paid today but he probably
won't show up again
My children are so good but that's probably
going to change

As each day passes by nothing is as it seems
I'm healthy but I'm surely going to die
Probably from one of the five things that
captures every life

I'm happy but I'm living with a disease
That captures every moment and adds an
ingredient of unease
It steals my life and makes it lame
Taking my joy before it even came

Lord I'm struggling, begging you on my knees
Help me let go of this ailment, doubt is my
disease

Renewed Mind

My mind is my best friend
It's also the thing that tries to do me in
When it's on, I feel that I can be all that I can be
When it's not, I feel so defeated

It keeps me there and says let's sit until I have plan
I need to think about this situation I've gotten myself
in
Then God says your mind won't figure it out
If it could defeat would have never come out

I must renew my mind each and everyday
I must renew it in God, the author of my faith
My mind alone will never be enough
It's highly functioning and equipped with some
powerful stuff

It likes to suck in the things it sees
Sadness and defeat are a powerful diseases
Making it physically hard to cope
God says I have the cure for your mind disease

It's not a pill or a class it's trusting in me
When you trust you believe and you know
That God is with you the protector of your soul
He protects your soul, and your soul should lead your
mind
Not the other way around else troubles you'll find
Feed your soul so it's strong and it can be
The thing that tells your mind constantly to believe

Please Help

What does it feel like when a dream dies
Its the death of hope in thinking that you can
achieve
The thing you wish for, the thing you dream
It's believing that it will never come true
That there are no options, no solutions to turn to
So I give my dead dream to you
Because at this point I don't know what to do
You told me that all things are possible through
you
So God please help me and show me what to do
Better yet please intervene on my behalf
Help me cope, show me a path to grab
I don't know if the dream is dead or the belief
that it come true
Lord please help, please help me make it through

Resting

Extreme Fatigue, I've been running for so long
My soul and heart aches so much, I'm having a
hard time pressing on
Running toward, running away, stopping to see
where I'm at
My tired spirit has had no place to rest

This weariness is settling into my soul
Weighing me down, slowing me, cause it has
caught ahold
I'm tired, I'm soo tired, I just want to be
Not weighed down so much with life's infirmities

I've tried, I've tried, so many avenues
Praying for directions, searching every corner,
looking for clues
I'm exhausted, how do I know God if it's really
you
I want to do your will but I just don't know
what to do

I can rest and not faint, if I remember his
provision
He'll walk with me, carry me, through every
possible condition

There's no weariness if I rest in the bosom of
the lord
Holding my faith as my shield and the word as
my sword

There's no burden, no situation that he can't
carry me through
Faith in him and him alone gives peace and
renews

I should be full and joyous of spirit in the midst
of a storm
Knowing God holds my soul close and safe from
harm

For his yolk is easy and his burden light
There's no need to be weighted down by the
trials and tribulations in life

For his word remains true, never changing ,
what he says will come to be
So standing in his word, resting in his arms is
where you'll find me

The Greatest Love of All

I was so proud of you today
You took a leap and stepped out on your faith
You thanked me and said thy will be done
You opened your heart and we became as one

You laid your head down at my feet
You cried out for mercy and that this moment won't
repeat
I fixed your circumstances and gave you a pass
I told you that your salvation will always last

I've watched you from afar and especially up close
Your beauty, your heart but your spirit I love the most
It's beautiful and whole and perfectly made
It became whole and perfect on the day you gave
Me all of you and held nothing back

Every heartache and pain, you let me have
I love you, you shared your burdens with me
You poured out your heart and my promises will
always come to be

So rest tonight and know I will always be there
Through it all because I will always care
My love will flow and be poured within
My love will sustain you even through your sin
My love will blanket and cover you
My love is the greatest and will always endure
My love is love, it's where love was created
My love sent my only begotten son
To reconnect us so that we can be as one

This connection is why I did what I did
An eternity of separation is not what I want to give
So know that my love will not waver or fall
There's nothing you did to earn it at all

So if you can't earn it, it won't be taken away
It's just my nature to love you anyway
So close your eyes and remember this prayer
Let it hold you close so you know that I'm there

Thank you for love that flows from above
Thank you for sending your only begotten son
I'll never fully understand your love for me
A broken being with so many imperfections
So I'm glad I can't do anything
I can't lose it nor can I gain it
It's there, even if I don't open my heart
It's there in my failings and when I fall short
It's there through my tears and my pain
It's there through the sunshine and rain
It was there in the beginning
And it will endure for all eternity
In Jesus name I thank and praise you for your love
Amen

God's Word

Feed me
While I'm full I'm still fainting from thirst
My appetite is sated but my soul cries the worst
Because if hasn't been fed for many many years
I come here every Sunday yet I find no nourishment
here

I thought this was supposed to be like an all you can
eat buffet
Where I go here with my church family, so we can
celebrate our faith
Where I swallow God's word because it's enough to fill
my cup
But when you cover it with foolishness and messiness
it makes me not want to pick it up

Gods word is not tainted
It's the purest food you can eat
You don't need to save it for special occasions
You don't need sides to go with the meat

God's word is the main dish
We choose to add the sides
Where we start to lose focus of what he can do in our
lives

God's word is everlasting
It stretches from the beginning to the end
It blankets me in his presence
It forgives me for my sins

God's word is the truth
It can't be twisted for gain
It really has all the nutrients
That I need to maintain
Not just to maintain my soul but to grow my faith ten
fold

It needs to fill me up until I overflow
Because in that over flowing
I have more of God to give
Because through my abundance they can see that God
lives

So I need to feed my soul each and every day
I won't let it get thirsty because that's when the devil
will say
Why do you keep eating food that doesn't satisfy you
I got something better for you to chew
Why do you keep returning time after time
You might as well let that thing die
Trust me you'll be just fine
Just feed your flesh until you're time is up

But my soul tells me I have more work to do
God says please know my word it has all the answers
to pull you through
My word will give you everything to endure

This famine of destruction across the land
The soulless ways that we see in your fellow man
God says don't worry I have a plan
So in his word I will stand

And I will allow him to always hold my hand
Because if he has it I know he'll never let go
I know this because his word told me so

Lightning Source UK Ltd.
Milton Keynes UK
UKHW021941280519
343492UK00004B/62/P